Quick Recovery

First Aid
for the
Jewish Soul

compiled by evelyn l. beilenson

illustrated by jo gershman

 Peter Pauper Press, Inc.
White Plains, New York

Visit us at
www.peterpauper.com

Designed by Heather Zschock

Portions of this compilation previously appeared in
Wit and Wisdom of Israel, edited by Elliot Beier.

Text copyright © 2000
Peter Pauper Press, Inc.
202 Mamaroneck Avenue
White Plains, NY 10601
Illustrations copyright © 2000
Jo Gershman
ISBN 0-88088-332-4
Printed in China
7 6 5 4 3 2 1

First Aid
for the
Jewish Soul

introduction

The Jewish soul has endured through the ages. First aid for the Jewish soul often comes in the form of the written word, be it the Talmud, the Midrash, or the thoughts of Jewish scholars, both traditional and modern. The Jews have always looked to "the book" for guidance and spiritual sustenance.

Most Jewish principles are timeless, and apply now as they did in days of old. They are not only philosophical but extremely practical.

We hope the words compiled in this book give the reader the inspiration often needed in times of stress and misfortune, as well as in times of joy.

E. L. B.

The world is new to us every
morning—this is God's gift;
and every man should believe
he is reborn each day.

• BAAL SHEM TOV •

[T]he unexplainable, the ultimately unknowable. . . . we call that something "spirit"—the spirit of this people—which has no limitations and is indestructible.

This spiritual strength is eternal. It is transmitted from generation to generation, almost unwittingly.

• GOLDA MEIR •

Only the lesson which is
enjoyed can be learned well.

• talmud •

A little light dispels
much darkness.

• ISSACHAR EILENBURG •

Being Jewish is the wellspring
of my inspiration. . . .
Living Jewish directs
me beyond the letter of the
law into its spirit.

• letty cottin pogrebin •

The Jewish heart has always
starved unless it was fed
through the Jewish intellect.

• HENRIETTA SZOLD •

I have learned much from my teachers, more from my colleagues, but most of all from my pupils.

• MAIMONIDES •

Everyone must have two pockets,
so that he can reach into the one
or the other, according to his needs.
In his right pocket are to be the words:
"For my sake was the world
created," and in his left:
"I am but dust and ashes."

• RABBI BUNAM •

Nothing is as liberating
as joy. It frees the mind and
fills it with tranquillity.

• REBBE NACHMAN OF BRESLOV •

A man should so live
that at the close of every
day he can repeat:
"I have not wasted my day."

• ZOHAR •

When Law came
into the world, freedom
came into the world.

• talmud •

Behold, how good and how
pleasant it is for brethren
to dwell together in unity!

• psalms •

Be not in a hurry like
the almond, first to blossom
and last to ripen.
Be rather like the mulberry,
last to blossom and
first to ripen.

• AHIKAR •

Even in Paradise,

it is not good to be alone.

• YIDDISH PROVERB •

*Judaism's emphasis on unity is
a crucial source of awareness for me:
it is the foundation of empathy and
connectedness; it is the principle that
expresses the integrity of existence.*

• MARCIA FALK •

If a lecture is not as
alluring to the audience as
a bride to her groom, you had
better not deliver it at all.

• SIMEON BEN LAKISH •

My pen is my harp and
my lyre; my library is my
garden and my orchard.

• JUDAH HA-LEVI •

Many candles can be
kindled from one candle
without diminishing it.

• talmud •

How can man be
merciful to others
Who is merciless himself?

• ABRAHAM HASDAI •

Your old men shall dream
dreams, your young men
shall see visions.

• JOEL •

That which has been is that
which shall be, And that which
has been done is that which shall
be done, And there is nothing
new under the sun.

• ECCLESIASTES •

When a person begs for food
and clothing, there must be no
investigation of his need, for we
are told: "When thou seest
the naked . . . cover him."

• talmud •

He who brings up
the child is to be called
its father, not he who
gave him birth.

• MIDRASH •

Let thine ears hear what
thy mouth speaketh.

• T. J. BERAKOT •

*If you drop gold
and books, pick up
first the books and
then the gold.*

• SEFER HASIDIM •

*It is wrong to suppress
the views of an opponent.
It is more fitting to
ponder their meaning.*

• JUDAH LOWE •

Three possessions
should you prize: a field,
a friend, and a book.

• hai gaon •

Let every person, in every
generation, think of himself
as a former slave, freed
from bondage in Egypt.

• HAGGADAH •

Thy friend has a friend,
and thy friend's friend has
a friend: be discreet.

• talmud •

The more life is a
rush the sooner
it is a blur.

• noah ben shea •

*A good name is
rather to be chosen
than great riches.*

• PROVERBS •

Life is not a
matter of extent,
But of content.

• STEPHEN S. WISE •

*Judaism has no dying god,
no embalming of dead bodies,
above all no slightest version of
death-instinct—"Choose life."*

• cynthia ozick •

A man can live without spices,

but not without wheat.

• talmud •

I think the Jews have some insight.

Make no images, imitate no God.

After all, in His field, the graphic arts,

He is pre-eminent.

Then let that One who made the tan

deserts and the blue Van Allen belt

and the green mountains of

New England be in charge of Beauty,

which He obviously understands,

and let man, who was full of

forgiveness at Jerusalem,

and full of survival at Troy,

let man be in charge of Good.

• GRACE PALEY •

People who have a religion should
be glad, for not everyone has the gift
of believing in heavenly things. . . .
[A] religion, it doesn't matter which,
keeps a person on the right path. It
isn't the fear of God but the upholding
of one's own honor and conscience.

• ANNE FRANK •

Set me as a seal upon thine heart,
as a seal upon thine arm: for love is
strong as death; jealousy is cruel as the
grave: the coals thereof are coals of fire,
which hath a most vehement flame.

• SONG OF SONGS •

The most beautiful thing we can
experience is the mysterious. It is the
source of all true art and all science.
He to whom this emotion is a stranger,
who can no longer pause to wonder
and stand rapt in awe, is as good
as dead: his eyes are closed.

• ALBERT EINSTEIN •

*Occupy yourself with
doing good, and the bad will
automatically fall away.*

• REBBE NACHMAN OF BRESLOV •

*If you cannot sound the depths
of the heart of man or unravel the
arguments of his mind, how can you
fathom the God who made
all things, or sound his mind or
unravel his purposes?*

• JUDITH •

[T]he family is the carrier of the covenant.
To maintain the partnership with
God and fulfill the responsibility in
the covenant, we have to have children
and pass the message and the tasks on.
What you can't do in your own
lifetime you expect the future
generations to do.
[T]he family is our wheel of life.

• BLU GREENBERG •

You feel oppressed by
your Judaism only
as long as you do not
take pride in it.

• BERTHA PAPPENHEIM •

Why snatch at wealth, and
hoard and stock it?
Your shroud, you know,
will have no pocket.

• BETTY PAOLI •

*A carpenter who has
no tools is not a carpenter.*

• talmud •

*In Judaism social
action is religiousness,
and religiousness implies
social action.*

• LEO BAECK •

It is better to grow wings
and fly away, than submit
to a godless king.

• ESTHER RABBAH •

To be a Jew is
a destiny.

• VICKI BAUM •

Pray only in a room
with windows [to remember
the world outside].

• talmud •

There are no doors,
there are no guards.
Through theological exploration
Judaism can belong to
all who desire it.

• SUSANNAH HESCHEL •

If I am not for myself,
who will be for me?
But if I am for myself only,
what am I?
And if not now, when?

• hillel •

Honor thy father and thy mother,

even as thou honorest God;

for all three have been

partners in thy creation.

• ZOHAR •

Ceremonies at the synagogue . . . ,
the lighting up of the Sabbath candles
at home on Friday evenings—
these are not, in themselves, all in all.
Rather, they are the keys that open
the gates for the flooding of the spirit
with the true verities . . .

• REBEKAH KOHUT •

Keep in mind that the essence
of your prayers is the faith
you have in them that they
will be answered.

• REBBE NACHMAN OF BRESLOV •

Whatsoever thy hand
finds to do, do it with
all thy might.

• ECCLESIASTES •

The motto should not be:
Forgive one another; rather,
understand one another.

• emma goldman •

All beginnings are difficult.

• mıdʀash •

The price of wisdom

is above rubies.

• JOB •

A soft answer turneth

away wrath.

• PROVERBS •

And Ruth said,

Intreat me not to leave thee,

or to return from following after thee:

for whither thou goest, I will go;

and where thou lodgest, I will lodge:

thy people shall be my people,

and thy God my God.

• Ruth •

To every thing there is
a season, and a time to every
purpose under heaven . . .

• ECCLESIASTES •

Strength and dignity are her clothing;
And she laugheth at the time to come.
She openeth her mouth with wisdom;
And the law of kindness is on her tongue.

• PROVERBS •

Love is the voice of God.

• GRACE AGUILAR •

Train up a child in the way he should go: and when he is old, he will not depart from it.

• PROVERBS •

Oh, deem not dead that martial fire,
Say not the mystic flame is spent!
With Moses' law and David's lyre,
Your ancient strength remains unbent.

• EMMA LAZARUS •
THE BANNER OF THE JEW